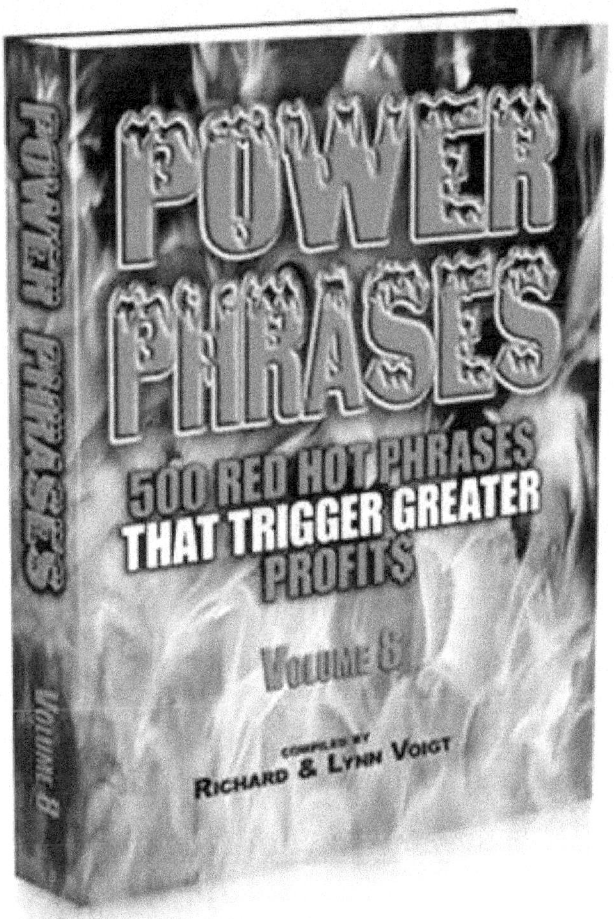

POWER PHRASES

500 RED HOT PHRASES THAT TRIGGER GREATER PROFIT$

VOLUME 8

COMPILED BY

RICHARD & LYNN VOIGT

POWER PHRASES – Vol. 8
500 Power Phrases That Trigger Greater Profits

ISBN-13: 978-1-940961-07-1
ISBN-10: 1940961076

First Printing, 2013

Printed in the United States of America

Income Disclaimer

This book contains educational materials meant to inspire ways to promote personal ideas, products and services that may be appropriate to incorporate or use in one's personal or business strategy, marketing method or any other related personal or business, that regardless of the author's results and experience, may not produce the same results (or any results) for you. The authors make absolutely no guarantee, either expressed or implied, that by implementing any ideas herein will gain success, make money, or improve current personal or business circumstances. There are simply far too many variable factors that come into play regarding any level of achievement or success in said personal and/or business venture. Primarily, results will depend on the nature of the product or business model, the conditions of the marketplace, the experience of the individual, and situations and elements that are beyond your control or that of the authors.

As with any business endeavor, you assume all risk related to investment and money based on your own discretion and at your own potential expense. If you intend to quote, copy, or use any content herein, in part or whole, it shall be the sole responsibility of the individual to be mindful of all active and lawfully protected copyrights, trademarks, and/or services-marks, by conducting due diligence prior to said usage.

Liability Disclaimer

This book is strictly intended for educational purposes only and was intended to inspire the individual to create ideas of their own design. This book represents the views of the authors as of the date of publication. Due to constant changing conditions facing the information age, the authors reserve the irrevocable right to modify and update their opinions based upon changing conditions. While the authors have made a "good faith" effort to verify the accuracy of information within this book, the authors or their affiliates/partners do not assume any liability or responsibility for inadvertent errors, omissions, or inaccuracies. This book is not intended to be used as a legal guide or resource, nor are the authors attempting to render any legal, accounting, theraputic, medical, or other professional services or advice. If said professional consultation or adivce is required, the authors recommend the reader immediately seek the services of a competent professional. It shall be the reader's responsibility to be fully aware of any and all federal, state, local or country laws that govern and/or affect personal or business transactions. Any slight of ethnicity, culture, gender, orientation, or existing organization as is any reference to persons or businesses, living or dead, is unintentional and purely coincidental.

Terms of Use

POWER PHRASES

Volume 8

500 POWER PHRASES THAT TRIGGER GREATER PROFITS

Compiled by
Richard & Lynn Voigt
I.M. Education Specialists

Introduction:

Powerful Phrases, Headlines, Sub Headlines, Slogans, Bullet Points and Interview Sound Bites are perhaps the most powerful marketing tools mankind has ever created. They are the lifeblood behind every business venture are the ultimate secret weapon of Millionaire Marketers.

No matter whether you are introducing or promoting a brand new product, teaching a "How To" skill, building a website, or simply sending an email, using the perfect power phrase is crucial to capturing and holding eyeballs and producing greater marketing profits.

In today's world every word you use has measurable impact. Each word can produce emotional psychological buttons that trigger psychological reactions. Successful advertisers understand that using an effective power phrase is a true art form that turns "wants" into instant gratification "needs." Once artfully triggered, any niche market can instantly create more protifable conversions.

Now it's your turn to personalize this incredible collection of 500 Power Phrases in ways that instantly advance your own effective marketing skills as you create new and power phrases, slogans, presentations, bullet points, or interview sound bites that take you to the next level.

Whether starting or running a small business, writing an ad, coming up with a memorable slogan, making a major corporate presentation, bullet points, creating a video, writing a book, searching for the perfect slogan, teaching a lesson or book report, your creative use of these Power Phrases can capture more eyeballs and produce some amazing rewards quickly turning you into a Marketing Genius. Now, it's your turn to make the magic happen!

POWER PHRASES

Volume 8 – 3501 - 4000

500 Power Phrases That Trigger Greater Profits

Begin Selecting & Customizing Your Perfect Marketing Phrase

3501	Refining Sell
3502	Master The Basics
3503	Valued Command Chain Locks In Profits
3504	Only 24 Hours Left
3505	By Joining Today You'll Receive
3506	More Customers Will Buy Your Product
3507	Never Have To Work Another Day Again
3508	Access Real World Promotions
3509	Wishing You Happiness Joy And Laughter
3510	Get On With It
3511	The Following Pages Will Make You Rich
3512	You'll Make Changes In Your Business After Reading This
3513	Does That Sound Good To You
3514	Value Equals Response
3515	Feeling Locked Out Of The Money Game
3516	Transform Sad Feelings Instantly
3517	Tune Into Source Energy
3518	Test Your Niche
3519	How Cool Is It Going To Work Now
3520	Make Lots Of Money With This Little Secret
3521	You're About To Create History

3522	**Are You A Millionaire Copywriter**
3523	**I'm Ready To Leave My Competition In The Dust**
3524	**Want To Partner With Incredible Tools Products And Services**
3525	**If You Could Pick Just One**
3526	**Learn Why It's Not Your Fault**
3527	**Gain Big Skills Fast**
3528	**Progress Limiting Phenomenon**
3529	**Almost *Force* People To Hand You Thick Wads Of Cash**
3530	**Super Charge The Process**
3531	**The Newest Cutting Edge Secrets Revealed Here**
3532	**This Program's Free**
3533	**Content Is The Lifeblood Of Our Business**
3534	**Backend Coaching**
3535	**Why Marketing Is Afraid Of The Truth**
3536	**Becoming A Gum Shoe**
3537	**Lion Or Lioness**
3538	**This Will Enable You To**
3539	**I'm The Only One Allowed To Promote This Product**
3540	**What Would It Look Like If It Was Perfect**
3541	**Incredible First Paragraph**
3542	**A Book Filled With Magic Bullets**
3543	**Launching Your Own Affiliate Program**
3544	**This Is An Incredible Marketplace**
3545	**The Answer Is Staring You In The Face**
3546	**Did I Say The Perfect Storm**
3547	**Truth Be Exposed**
3548	**I Recommend You Put Yourself Into This Program**
3540	**Revenue Producing Activity**
3550	**Harvest Open Source Collaboration**
3551	**I Felt Mine Was The Worst**
3552	**Are You Ready To Rise To A Brand New Day**
3553	**Every Word Is Important**
3554	**What's Your Field Intelligence**
3555	**Here Are Your Free Safelist Submitters**
3556	**What You Don't Need To Know**
3557	**Let's Get Back To Value**
3558	**Cash In On Education**
3559	**Earn Bonus Points Each Time You...**

3560	Why Marketers Don't Want You To Read This
3561	Want A Free $197 Consultation
3562	Are You Waiting Around For A Bailout
3563	The Dark Side Of Being Negative
3564	Want A Free $297 WP Security Update For Free
3565	Paint Your Dreams
3566	Prospecting Task Force
3567	For Those Who Say They Want More But Still Do Nothing
3568	Learn To Market Online
3569	Instant Results
3570	Why You Need To Be Direct And Clear
3571	Sorry I'm Late
3572	Recognizing Superfluous Barriers
3573	Request The Best
3574	Your Private Invitation To The Biggest Sale Of The Year
3575	Zero Marginal Costs
3576	Processing Dot Dot Dot
3577	Persuasive Sabotage Taps Into A Fortune
3578	Fast Friday Fancies
3579	Here Are Some Of The Results
3580	Why An Open Color Works Best
3581	We All Need To Play
3582	But Hey - It's Your Life
3583	Information Is Great But
3584	I've Yet Come Up For Air
3585	You Don't Have To Wait
3586	Do You Know What The Internet Is For
3587	Consider Gel Or Mousse
3588	Gardening Is Therapeutic
3589	Don't Believe Fake Screenshots
3590	Great Systems Succeed
3591	I've Received Emails Begging Access For This
3592	Launching Rockets Of Desire
3593	More Sales For Your Business
3594	Stable Reliable Trustworthy
3595	Call To Action Headlines Snatch Your Reader's Attention
3596	How To Create New Ideas
3597	The Wealth Revolution Is Here

3598	How To Stop Short Of Your Dreams
3599	What You Can Do Now
3600	Don't Put Undo Pressure On Yourself
3601	It's Hip To Be Square
3602	Nothing Stands In Your Way
3603	Have They Traveled The Path You're About To Take
3604	How Long Have You Been A Member
3605	The Color Of Your Money
3606	Ultimate Control Of Your Income Potential
3607	A Few Clicks Of Your Mouse And It's Done
3608	Can You Pass The Secret Test
3609	Want To See Where The Future Is Headed
3610	Related Niches For Cross Promotion
3611	One Little Bit Left
3612	I'm Going To Show You How To Do This
3613	New Products Dominate The Economy
3614	Populate Your Spreadsheet
3615	Click The Order Button
3616	Follow Through With Voice Projection
3617	Research Takes Time And Money
3618	Hitting Psychological Triggers
3619	The Kiss Test
3620	Rare Hidden Traits
3621	Betting On Small Business
3622	Drink From The Fire Hose Of Successful Marketing
3623	Are You On The Endangered List
3624	Our Crazy Marketing Quilt
3625	Are You Heading For The Dark Side
3626	Calling The Networks
3627	Be Aware Of This Shifting Marketplace Niche
3628	Flip It On Its Head
3629	Take A Good Look At This Update
3630	Do The Full Review
3631	Little Biz Big Money
3632	Three Question Evoke Startling Epiphany
3633	I'm Keeping This Offer Valuable And Extremely Limited
3634	Too Much Too Little Just Right
3635	I'll Do It For You

3636	**Target Your Market With Laser Precision**
3637	**The Story Going On In Their Head**
3638	**Producing Digital Only Versions**
3639	**No Fancy Sales Talk Here**
3640	**Discover The Benefits Of Mobile Marketing**
3641	**The Interpreneur Saves Their Company**
3642	**Only Buy What You Want**
3643	**Make Sure You Have A Dreamer In Your Organization**
3644	**Resale Rights Product Library**
3645	**Cash Back Fast**
3646	**Slip Into The Right Mindset**
3647	**Examples Of Niche Markets You Can Look Into**
3648	**My Best Product For Free**
3649	**Repeat What You're Doing And Expand Your Business Efforts**
3650	**It Disappeared Overnight**
3651	**Take Your Ranking To The Next Level**
3652	**Can You Make Me A List Of 10 Creative Ideas**
3653	**Grow To Be Heard**
3654	**Acute Pain Isn't Cute**
3655	**The Single Most Misunderstood Way To Make Money Online**
3656	**What We Recommend You Consider**
3657	**We Almost Came To A Brawl When It Happened**
3658	**Bring Your Gifts Out In The Open**
3659	**Find New And Rare Things**
3660	**Separating Theory From Truth**
3661	**Listen And Observe**
3662	**Without This I Failed Miserably**
3663	**Mightier Than The Rejections**
3664	**Take The EZ Wealth Tour**
3665	**Tactics That Really Matter To Customers**
3666	**Schwing Ding**
3667	**Unless You're Superman You Couldn't Possibly Do It**
3668	**We Just Change The Access Code**
3669	**Satisfy Your Needs Now**
3670	**Come And Get It**
3671	**Take Advantage Of Your Peak Time**
3672	**Coin A Phrase That Gets Notice**
3673	**Her Love Rules The Internet**

3674	What's Keeping You Poor
3675	Never Look At It Again
3676	Conduct Thorough Keyword Research Early
3677	Create More Buy Buttons
3678	Leap Over The Corporate Ladder
3679	You Can Be My Wingman Any Time
3680	Just Like You
3681	They Told Me I Shouldn't Do This
3682	Credit Crisis
3683	Taking You Deep Inside
3684	Moving Fast Because You Need To
3685	Think Of Your Headline As An Ad For Your Ad
3686	Screw The Economy This Idea Is Better
3687	Opening The Door For The Coming Year
3688	Physical vs. Emotional Pain
3689	No One Knows What We Do
3690	Welcome Marketers Advertisers And Affiliates
3691	Close Your Eyes And Inhale
3692	Valuable Lessons For Improvement
3693	How Many Chances Do You Need
3694	Customer Appreciation Coupon
3695	Even Blind Squirrels Find Nuts Once In A While
3696	Revolutionize The Digital Download Industry
3697	Reach Hungry Customers And Get Guaranteed Traffic
3698	You'll Need Dry Shorts For This
3699	Be Very Smart Going In
3700	Did You Produce A Video
3701	Unlimited Access Available
3702	Why You'll Never Beat Me At Scrabble
3703	Defining A Clearer Vision For Your Success
3704	Yes It's That Easy
3705	What Can I Do That People Can't Live Without
3706	The Biggest Problem Is Processing All The Money
3707	Intelligence Is Dynamic
3708	Tool For Discovery Used In Marketing
3709	In The Spotlight Now
3710	The Creative Class
3711	Three Goals Of A Business

3712	**Created By Us Just For You And Your Friends**
3713	**The Buy Button Is About To Disappear**
3714	**Really All This And Starting At Just One Green Dollar**
3715	**I Met Someone Who Changed My Life Forever**
3716	**Are You A Real Person On Video**
3717	**Just Pure Salesmanship**
3718	**Tell Me Something I Don't Know**
3719	**This Is Way Too Important**
3720	**Must Have A Specific Offer**
3721	**Write A Self-Help Book**
3722	**Stand Out Dynamically From Your Niche**
3723	**Powerfully Teaching One Thing**
3724	**How Much Defends Upon You**
3725	**You'll Understand Why This Is Available Today Only**
3726	**How Keyword Density Impacts Your Page Rank**
3727	**My Inbox Is Jammed**
3728	**Invest In Virtual Real Estate**
3729	**This Is So Impressive It Will Destroy The Marketing Paradigm**
3730	**OK It's Your Turn Now**
3731	**Cloning Your Own Possibilities**
3732	**Style Guide To Success**
3733	**Will It Get Worse**
3734	**Achieve A Different Reality**
3735	**Getting Your Corner Stones In Place**
3736	**Frame It From The Advantage**
3737	**Push On Your Pleasure Centers**
3738	**You're Being Ripped Off**
3739	**Huge Thumbs Up**
3740	**Why Would You Want To Do That**
3741	**Recession Busting Ideas**
3742	**Weed Out The Losers**
3743	**We're Waiting For You**
3744	**This Course Will Help You To Avoid Failure**
3745	**Trend Data**
3746	**We'd Like To Start Placing Customers Under You**
3747	**Article Marketing Research For Your Niche**
3748	**Found Myself Questioning Everything**
3749	**Keep It Authentic And Moving**

3750	**Here's What Success Means To Me**
3751	**Sleepy Sunday Secrets**
3752	**A Knowledge Based Economy**
3753	**Good News Galore**
3754	**Writing Headlines Can Be Sticky**
3755	**Custom Web Programming**
3756	**Congratulate Yourself For Doing This**
3757	**Visual Process Maps**
3758	**Get A Surprise**
3759	**Show It To Me Right Now**
3760	**Where Do You Want To Go**
3761	**Tap Into Thousands**
3762	**Simple Screenshots**
3763	**Be Sure There's A Demand**
3764	**The #1 Wealth Builder**
3765	**Want The Whole Scoop**
3766	**The Holy Grail Of Marketing**
3767	**What I Have Is The Solution**
3768	**Whack Them On Your iPod**
3769	**Tell Their Story Not Yours**
3770	**What Emotion Do You Want To Create**
3771	**Why I Wanted A Copy**
3772	**Ciao Bella**
3773	**101 Tips**
3774	**Do A Once Over Before Presenting**
3775	**It's An Immediate Free Download**
3776	**Let Me Share A Little Example**
3777	**Who Are You**
3778	**Your Headline Will Make Or Break You**
3779	**Committed To Results**
3780	**Only 8 Emails And No More**
3781	**It's Extremely Important That You Secure Your License Now**
3782	**Money-Making Internet Business In Steroid Heaven**
3783	**Want Some Valuable Information**
3784	**Reward Yourself**
3785	**Get Your Product Out There Fast**
3786	**Stand Back And Admire The Answer**
3787	**Reinforce Their Problem**

3788	Is Your Marketing Forecast Stormy
3789	I'm Going To Ride It One More Time
3790	Are Your Emails Being Delivered Opened And Clicked
3791	Honest And Profitable
3792	Don't Try Harder Try Easier
3793	I've Never Liked The Odds
3794	Achieve Your Full Potential
3795	Scientific Advertising
3796	If I Could Just Do This
3797	The Marketing Zombie Apocalypse
3798	Use These Tools To Get A Feel
3799	Infects The Masses
3800	Mobile Solution
3801	License Your Product To Me
3802	Need A Different Perspective
3803	The Answer Is Simple Time Equals Money
3804	Hypnotic Squeeze Pages
3805	Settling For Scraps
3806	I Want Buyers Not Just A List
3807	The Greatest Of All Time
3808	Meeting Your Quota
3809	Needed Cash Injection
3810	This Isn't Some Kind Of Sales Gimmick
3811	My Must-Read List
3812	Grab A Huge Discount Right Now
3813	The Big Light Bulb In My Head
3814	Ultra High Quality
3815	Body Language Moves Your Audience
3816	Thousands Of People Want To Get Their Hands On These
3817	Is Your eCommerce Biz Providing You Significant Growth
3818	The Secret To Building A Massive Financial Success
3819	It's All About The Traffic
3820	How Success Become Self-Perpetuating
3821	Proven Success Lessons
3822	Why It Takes So Long To Create A Product
3823	Your Own Electronic Mail Slave
3824	Crushes Your Competition Into A Thousand Tiny Pieces
3825	Applying New Methods

3826	Don't Lead Yourself Down The Wrong Path
3827	Share Your Results
3828	Hot Ways To Sell Your Products Like Crazy
3829	Earn An Extra 3000 Points Today Only
3830	Cutting Edge Technology Is Available For Beta Testing
3831	Learn 12 Basic Secrets Of A Successful Business
3832	Scrape Up True Grit
3833	You Like Special Deals Don't You
3834	Can You Model That Business
3835	A Professional Blogger's Check List
3836	Join On Online Panel
3837	Don't Wait Too Long
3838	What Dogs Need Is People Training
3839	Simply Attribute Contributing Resources
3840	Gain That Self Confidence You've Desired
3841	The Most Important Part Of Living
3842	Why Follow The Corporate Ladder
3843	Old Time Talk
3844	Listening Is An Art - But Action Is The Answer
3845	Seeking Creative Solutions
3846	Ancient Language
3847	Establishing Page Quality Videos
3848	Conquer Fear Through Knowledge
3849	Things Weren't Looking Good
3850	Easy Reasons For Failure
3851	Why Others Are Eavesdropping
3852	You Got Any More Of Those
3853	Hot New Advertising Program Delivers
3854	Feel Completely Lost And Isolated
3855	Stop Read And Learn
3856	Find And Create Hot Topic Products
3857	Access The Bonus Area
3858	Customers Every Single Day
3859	Your Mail Is Being Sent
3860	If You Didn't Care You Wouldn't Be Here
3861	Get Out Of The Way Of Success
3862	A Marketing Pandemic Will Soon Be Set Free
3863	Big Turn Around Makeovers That Will Change Your Life

3864	**Factories No More**
3865	**When It's Perfectly Wrong**
3866	**Cash In On New Product Trends**
3867	**Got A Second To Make A Fortune**
3868	**Gain Invaluable Insight Into This Unique Opportunity**
3869	**Not Just More Stuff**
3870	**Solving The Attrition Problem**
3871	**Want Traffic Cash**
3872	**Playing To Win Or Waiting To Fail**
3873	**Christmas Cash Flow**
3874	**Can Never Make Enough Eye Contact**
3875	**Brand New Potential Profit Center**
3876	**Your Knowledge Give You An Advantage**
3877	**Supercharge Your Ability To Communicate**
3878	**Only Wishing You Could**
3879	**Let Me Explain**
3880	**Five Places Where You Can Find New Products To Sell**
3881	**Quiet And Make Your Fears Disappear**
3882	**Create A Killer OTO**
3883	**What Other Slants Can Your Find Tweak And Exploit**
3884	**Create Your Own Automated Income Stream**
3885	**Amazing Free Offer Will Skyrocket Your Traffic**
3886	**Lack Of Income Is No Big Deal**
3887	**Lack Of Content Loses Them**
3888	**Turn It Into A Monster Product**
3889	**Be The Envy Of Your Marketing Neighborhood**
3890	**Hype vs. Exaggeration**
3891	**Who's Your Favorite Cartoon Character**
3892	**What An Amazing Lineup**
3893	**Flying Off The Digital Shelf**
3894	**Request Your Free Bonuses**
3895	**Who Is The Most Innovative Person You Know**
3896	**No More Thuds**
3897	**Spoon Fed Money Making Ideas**
3898	**Thanks For Downloading Our Offer**
3899	**Why Writing Sales Letters Is So Hard**
3900	**No Skills No Experience No Excuse**
3901	**Make A Great Gift**

3902	Post Unlimited Ads
3903	Free And Paid Channels
3904	These Tools Are Highly Effective
3905	Just Making Sure
3906	Successful Cookie Cutters
3907	Key To Continued Success
3908	I Want To Hear More
3909	Time Spacialization Skills
3910	Promise Of The Future
3911	Still Questioning What To Supply
3912	Keep Your Body Serif Fonts
3913	We're Not Stopping Development
3914	Now You Can And Now You Will
3915	Outstanding System You Must Use
3916	Setting Your Short Term Goals
3917	Can Copy And Content Co-Mingle
3918	Offer These And No One Will Ask For A Refund
3919	There's Too Much Information
3920	A Priceless Experience You'll Never Forget
3921	Become Part Of Something Real
3922	Behind The Scene Search Engine Optimization
3923	Proven Educational Platform
3924	What Kind Of Experience Is Needed
3925	WARNING Your Personal Information Is Being Sold
3926	Future Millionaire
3927	These Prices Will Cause Them To Switch
3928	People Do Judge Authors By Their Covers
3929	Fast And Furious Headlines
3930	This Opportunity Is Yours For The Taking
3931	Consider Setting A Physical Reason For Shutting Down An Offer
3932	Are Your Customers Paying Promptly Enough
3933	Your Best Testimonial Is Yours
3934	Giving You More Money
3935	Your Children Get Only One Childhood
3936	Do You Really Want To Struggle Online Year After Year
3937	Select The Right Topic
3938	I Fully Endorse This System
3939	Digital Product Management

3940	**No Overhead And Definitely No Pile Of Stuff**
3941	**What To Creatively Change In Your Life**
3942	**Why The Right Tools Are So Vital To Your Business**
3943	**The Naked Truth About Me And You**
3944	**Provide A Thank You**
3945	**Breaking News Story**
3946	**Start Charging More For Your Same Products Or Services**
3947	**What's Your Current Strength**
3948	**Unlimited Upload Capacity**
3949	**Map Out Every Task And Destroy Potential Problems**
3950	**I Want To Help Them Get That Done**
3951	**Designed To Earn Monthly Income For Life**
3952	**A Whole New Mind**
3953	**[ORDER HERE]**
3954	**What's Education Really For**
3955	**Most People Don't Want To Buy This**
3956	**You Really Should Check It Out**
3957	**Ads That Stick In Your Mind**
3958	**Get Awesome Footage**
3959	**Excess Inventory**
3960	**Find 10 Different Markets Then Focus On Only One**
3961	**You'll Want To Chose This Option**
3962	**Will Truly Amaze You**
3963	**Times Are Changing Every Nano Second**
3964	**Create Projects With The Ultimate Advantage**
3965	**Reach Brand New People**
3966	**Can You Make It With Search Marketing**
3967	**That's Not Even The Whole Story**
3968	**No Prescription Necessary**
3969	**Now A Devoted Believer**
3970	**Is Your Money Passing You By**
3971	**Marketing Knows No Boundaries**
3972	**A Great Optional Strategy**
3973	**Actually That's A Lie**
3974	**Spikes That Come Out Of Nowhere**
3975	**Telling Lots Of Stories**
3976	**Resources To Generate More Revenue Online**
3977	**Win Higher Page Rank**

3978	Drown All Your Sorrows
3979	No More Scheduled Meetings
3980	Clean Up Everything Around You
3981	How Can You Tell Which Products Sell
3982	Snap Your Fingers
3983	Change The System Not The Symptom
3984	A Grotesque Understatement
3985	Your Income Will Compound
3986	Take In Information
3987	I Found Your Wallet
3988	Auction Off Your Skills
3989	My Blog Is Cruising
3990	Hands Free Web Page
3991	Sponsor These Great Brands
3992	The Snowball Effect
3993	Moving Forward To Prosperity
3994	Charging High Margins
3995	It's Important How You Phrase Things
3996	It's What You Do Next That Counts
3997	Access The Web From Your Phone
3998	Explore Deep Space Of Internet Marketing
3999	This Back End Logic Makes Things Happen Fast
4000	The Best Possible Way To Start

Lynn and I hope that this "Think Tank" volume series of 500 Hot Phrases will helped you clearly paint your dreams, sell your ideas, and market your messages, propelling each of your ideas and projects toward incredible success. Watch for our next Volume!

We truly wish you the very best and look forward to hearing your success stories.

Concluding Thoughts:

Ever success is built upon a preparing a strong foundation, having a clear vision, and taking positive action each and every day. If you've been searching for a new lifestyle, then you'll find this book directive and inspirational. You can open it to any page and let that page help you rethink possibilities, consider new ideas, open new opportunities, and ultimately experience a more successful and fulfilling lifestyle.

Every problem has a solution! Regardless of your current situation or circumstance, know that you have the power and responsibility to redirect your life in any direction you choose. Simply start thinking about and research the kind of lifestyle that truly appeals to your heart. Begin your new journey by learning everything you can about your chosen subject. When you make that commitment, you'll open more unexpected doors to unique opportunities than imagined.

**"Creative Thought Is The Only Reality
Everything Else Is Merely The By-Product Of That Thought."**
- Walter Russell

So why not start thinking **BIGGER? It won't cost you any more.** It all starts by never allowing your current life's situation, environment, or so-called friends to limit your path to a happier, healthier, and successful life. After all, whose life is this?

Make a decision to focus on learning something new each and every day. Begin attracting your ideal lifestyle by doing something you love and enjoy. As difficult as it may be, don't allow money to limit your dreams. Focus on the kind of thoughts that make you feel good. Once you learn how to control your focus, you'll have a great chance to see your dreams take shape. You've finally learn to harness the power you always had within, a Universal Energy stream that flows 365/24/7 in any direction your project your thoughts, Good or Bad. Want proof? The thoughts you currently believe and project reflect the life you're currently living. Therefore, if your life isn't happening, change your thoughts, and change your life. It's something only you can hold, visualize, and project, living your dream come true.

Find yourself a mentor and spend more time with people who truly appreciate, support, and foster your dreams. Life may be short, but the thoughts we hold can make our life wider and more fulfilling.

About The Authors:

Richard and Lynn develop creative strategies that paint dreams, sell ideas, & market messages Together, they present a unique team-approach, working side-by-side, helping clients pursue their passions while sharing their skills and diverse expertise as authors, artists, inventors, entrepreneurs, & Internet marketing education specialists.

Teaching by example, they mentor proven self-publishing services, graphic design, video production, domain acquisition, and marketing research of behalf of their company, RIVO Inc – RIVO Marketing, since 1997. They've created & produced hundreds of videos, self-published dozens of books on a wide variety of topics and created thousands of original works of fine art, while refining their Internet Marketing techniques, mentoring programs, and related business website development.

Their mission is to continually uncover new products and services, test new strategies, and network useful solutions with off and online entrepreneurs, small business owners, writers, local artists, models, teachers, students, and marketing professionals.

Their goal is to help clients create an action plan that discovers and connects the missing pieces of the success puzzle. The goals they foster create multiple streams of income for today's volatile economic climate. Their motto is: "Do the work once and allow the work to create additional streams of income for a lifetime."

Feel free to contact them if you have questions or would like to tap into their talents and expertise. They appreciate your feedback and look forward to hearing your success stories.

Contact:
Richard & Lynn Voigt - RIVO
I. M. Education Specialists

RIVO INC - RIVO Marketing
13720 West Keefe Avenue
Brookfield, Wisconsin 53005 – USA
Email: support@RIVOinc.com
Website: www.RIVObooks.com
Website: www.WisconsinGarden.com

Visit Lynn's Garden: **www.WisconsinGarden.com**
view hundreds of great garden video blogs Tips

See Richard's Unique Artwork: **www.RIVOart.com**
view over 3,000 original Fine-Art compositions

Our Book Titles Now Available On Amazon:

THE GOLDEN VAULT OF MOTIVATIONAL QUOTATIONS
Words of Wisdom from The Greatest Minds & Leaders

BABY NAME .ME - 21,400 Names & Nicknames
For Family, Friends, Pets, Natural & Man-Objects

DOODLE DESIGNS Volumes 1-3
For Professionals & Kids Of All Ages
DOODLE DESIGNS – Vol. 1
DOODLE DESIGNS – Vol. 2
DOODLE DESIGNS Coloring Book Vol. 3

Work MORE Accomplish LESS Get FIRED!

ACTION HEADLINES That Drive Emotions – Volumes 1- 6
Paint Dreams, Sell Ideas & Market Your Message
Action Headlines That Drive Emotions Vol. 1
Action Headlines That Drive Emotions Vol. 2
Action Headlines That Drive Emotions Vol. 3
Action Headlines That Drive Emotions Vol. 4
Action Headlines That Drive Emotions Vol. 5
Action Headlines That Drive Emotions Vol. 6

IDIOMS – IDIOMS - IDIOMS
6,450 Popular Expressions That Put Words In Your Mouth

The CLICHÉ BIBLE - 8,400 Clichés For Sports Fanatics
& Lovers Of Popular Expressions

MORE THAN WORDS
5000+ Marketing Phrases That Sell

HYPNOTIC PHRASING
WARNING-This Book Teaches You How To Grab Eyeballs

YOUR RIGHT TO WEALTH
Becoming Wealthy Isn't Hard When You Know How

WI GARDEN – Let's Get Dirty
Our Wisconsin Garden Guide Promoting Delicious, Healthier Home-Grown Fresh Food, With Tools, Tips, & Ideas That Inspire Gardeners!

MONETIZE YOUR SOCIAL LIFE
Earn Extra Income While Having Fun Online

BABY NAMES
21,400 Unique Baby Names & Nicknames

FUNNY HEADLINES vol. 1
3,500 Outrageous Silly Brain Toots

FUNNY HEADLINES vol. 2
3,500 Outrageous Silly Brain Toots

JOBS
10,240 Career Paths That Can Change Your Life!

MONEY WORDS
Powerful Phrases That Million Dollar Copywriters Use To Make Piles Of Cash On Demand!

GARDEN QUOTATIONS
400 Garden Quotes From The Earth To Your Soul

HEADLINE STARTERS
175,000 Words That Paint Dreams, Sell Ideas, And Market Your Message

BABY NAMES
25,350 Baby Names & Nicknames For Your Family Friends & Pets
697 pages 7,000 Names with Origin & Meaning plus Top 100 Names, And 2,000 Most Popular Names

CURIOUS WORDS
15,800 Words That Expand Your Mind And Change Your Life

INSPIRING THOUGHTS
That Inspire Happiness, Success & A Clearer Understanding Of Life

MARKETING EYEBALLS
100 Ideas That Can Add Unlimited Subscribers To Your Lists

SECOND OF FIVE
My Early Years- From Birth To High School

POWER PHRASES – Individual Volumes 1 - 10
500 Power Phrases That Trigger Greater Profits

POWER PHRASES Pro Edition – Volumes 1-10 (Complete Series)
5000 Power Phrases That Trigger Greater Profits

COMING SOON! – BE THE FIRST TO GRAB YOUR PRO COPY

POWER PHRASES Pro Edition Volumes 1-10 (Complete Series)
5000 Power Phrases That Trigger Greater Profits

What do Marketing Millionaires know that you don't? They know how to pull money out of thin air by using their secret language of Power Phrases.

This Pro Edition of 5000 Red Hot Power Phrases not only saves you time and money but will help jump-start your creative brain in ways you may have never considered. Simply open this amazing collection to any page and find your perfect power phrase. All it may take is simply adding or replacing ONE word. It's simple, quick, and easy!

1. **Want to create more powerful profitable campaign offers?**
2. **Thinking of revitalizing a more professional business identity?**
3. **Want to update old product or service media advertisements?**
4. **Searching for fresh ideas that could improve sales and profits?**
5. **Looking for brand new ways to create stronger media sales copy?**
6. **Ready to use millionaire strategies advancing you to the next level?**

5000 POWER PHRASES is exclusively for professional Internet Marketers, authors,advertisers, executives, business owners, TV & radio reporters, entrepreneurs, administrators, managers, supervisors, teachers and students who want to find and access unique phrases for marketing slogans, presentation bullet points, and interview sound bites that powerfully paint dreams, sell ideas, and market your message.

Stop wasting valuable time, money, and energy racking your brain for new ideas. Create more profitable power phrase marketing campaigns for all your products, services, slogans, bullet points, and interview sound bites that finally grab and hold people's attention and trigger greater profits?

You now have a very powerful and professional marketing tool in your hand. We are confident that you know how to use it wisely in order to maximize the potential of all your marketing campaigns! Lynn and I **Thank You** for your support and purchase.

CLAIM 500 MORE POWER PHRASES!

Thank you for purchasing this eBook and in doing so we would like to send you **500 More Red Hot Power Phrases for FREE!**

When you post a **positive review of this Book on Amazon Books** under this title you'll receive an additional **500 POWER PHRASES.** Your review may also be sent directly to us.

Your request must be received within 30-days of purchase. Once your positive Book review is posted and verified, simply email the following to **(500@RIVOinc.com)**:

1. Full Name of Purchaser
2. Email address
3. Paypal Invoice Number
4. Copy of your posted Book Review*

Once we receive the above, we'll send you 500 Power Phrases **(PDF)** emailed to the address you provided.

Visit: www.RIVObooks.com for additional volumes as they become available including the Pro Edition of 5000 Red Hot Power Phrases that say what you mean to say and trigger greater profits.

Lynn and I look forward to your written comments and suggestions as we love hearing from each of our readers.

Richard & Lynn Voigt
RIVO Inc – RIVO Marketing
13720 West Keefe Avenue
Brookfield, Wisconsin 53005 USA
Telephone: (262) 783-5335
www.RIVObooks.com

P. S. If you love gardening, catch us on www.WisconsinGarden.com

***NOTE**: This offer is valid providing it does not violate the terms of service of the entity with whom you made this purchase. Duplicate or incomplete entries will also not be eligible and this offer is limited to one request per email address. All eligible review submissions become the property of RIVO Inc - RIVO Marketing – RIVO books and may be used as promotional testimonials ads on RIVO Inc websites. This offer may be withdrawn at any time without prior written notice.

www.ingramcontent.com/pod-product-compliance
Lightning Source LLC
LaVergne TN
LVHW010108110826
845155LV00028B/552

* 9 7 8 1 9 4 0 9 6 1 0 7 1 *